Haikus
FOR Jews

Also by David M. Bader

How to Be an Extremely Reform Jew

Haikus FOR Jews

For You, A Little Wisdom

David M. Bader

Harmony Books　New York

Published by Harmony Books, 201 East 50th Street, New York,
New York 10022. Member of the Crown Publishing Group.

Random House, Inc. New York, Toronto,
London, Sydney, Auckland

www.randomhouse.com

Harmony Books is a registered trademark of Random House, Inc.

Design by Barbara Sturman

Printed in the United States of America

Library of Congress Cataloging-in-Publication Data
Bader, David M.
    Haikus for Jews : for you, a little wisdom / David M. Bader.
        p.   cm.
    1. Jewish wit and humor.   2. Jews—Humor.   3. Senryu,
American.   4. Haiku, American.   I. Title.
    PN6231.J5B227   1999
    811'.041088924—dc21   99-31954
                                                  CIP

ISBN 0-609-60502-X

10 9 8

First Edition

Acknowledgments

The author thanks Jessica Schulte and her colleagues at Harmony Books; Patty Brown and John and Carol Boswell of John Boswell Associates; and kibitzing attorney-at-law Benjamin E. Rosenberg, Esq. He is also grateful to his parents, who taught him brevity by constantly interrupting. The author accepts all blame for any mistakes. Complaints should be submitted in the traditional 5-7-5 format.

There is no subject whatever

that is not fit for haiku.

—BASHO

This you call poetry?

—YIDDISH PROVERB

Foreword

Of all the many forms of Jewish-Japanese poetry, the Jewish haiku is perhaps the most sublimely beautiful. Consisting of just seventeen syllables, this little-known style of verse combines the simplicity and elegance of Asian art with the irritability and impatience of Jewish kvetching. Its brief, carefully wrought lines are designed to produce in the reader a "haiku moment"—a sudden, intense realization, such as "So that's it?"

The modern haiku owes its origins to fifteenth-century Japan, where it was first noticed that a seventeen-syllable poem was over much sooner than other poems. After the failure of experiments with eighteen- and nineteen-syllable alternatives ("too bloated"), the haiku was embraced by Zen masters and Samurai warrior monks, who were extremely pressed for time. In keeping with the era's rigid code of Bushido, haiku poets who exceeded the seventeen-syllable limit were given the choice of committing hara-kiri—ritual suicide—or apologizing for being so long-winded.

The earliest Jewish haikus were the contribution of the now almost-forgotten Jewish Haiku Mavens. Like the Japanese haiku, the Jewish haiku was typically an untitled work, consisting of three lines of five, seven, and five syllables, respectively.

It also had to include a *kigo,* or "season word," hinting at the time of year. For example, in traditional Japanese haiku, *russet* could suggest autumn, *dragonfly* could mean summer, while *cherry blossom* might connote spring. Similarly, in Jewish haiku, *sunblock* could signify summer, *extra sweater* winter, and *doing my taxes* spring. In Jewish haiku, the season word was sometimes left out entirely and replaced by a "home-furnishings word," such as *broadloom.*

Perhaps the most brilliant poet of the Jewish haiku was Sheldon "Sashimi" Lepstein, according to his mother. Lepstein grew up aspiring to be a retainer in the court of the Tokugawa Shogunate. Since he was born on the Upper West Side of Manhattan in 1948, he enrolled in City College instead. There, influenced by such haiku poets as Basho, Issa, and Shiki, he soon found himself drawn to the works of Melvin Weintraub (*"Floop, floop! The sound of / matzoh balls plunging into / boiling chicken broth"*) and Irving Gittelman (*"Pans empty, plates cleared, / yet another pot roast is / now indigestion"*).

Lepstein eventually mastered the intricacies of the Jewish haiku himself. Some of his finest efforts, the product of bitter life experience, were even more pointed and concise than traditional haiku, such as his searing one-syllable poem, *"Oy!"* and his two-syllable epic, *"Gevalt!"* He is perhaps best remembered today for the melancholy haiku

No fins, no flippers,

the gefilte fish swims with

some difficulty.

Though adhering to the traditional format, the haikus in this volume have been made more accessible to meet the needs of Jewish people who may be in a hurry. All syllables have been counted and re-counted by the accounting firm of PricewaterhouseCoopers. The author takes full responsibility for any errors that may have crept in, possibly as a result of proofreading after a heavy meal and feeling a little sleepy.

Haikus
FOR Jews

Five thousand years a

wandering people—then we

found the cabanas.

Hey! Get back indoors!

Whatever you were doing

could put an eye out.

$\mathcal{I}$n the ice sculpture

reflected bar-mitzvah guests

nosh on chopped liver.

How soft the petals

of the floral arrangement

I have just stolen.

Shocking new finding—

all this worrying really

will give you cancer.

$\mathcal{C}$atskills hotel sign—

PRESIDENT JOHNSON SLEPT HERE

Haven't changed a thing.

20
5
21

Add cholesterol,

overcook, then serve with bread—

recipe revealed.

Beyond Valium,®

the peace of knowing one's child

is an internist.

Firefly steals into

the night just like my former

partner, that gonif.

The same kimono

the top geishas are wearing—

got it at Loehmann's.

In a stage whisper

a yenta confides the name

of her friend's disease.

$\mathcal{N}$ew, at Oys "R" Us!

Hypochondriac Barbie

has a gout attack.

Jewish triathlon—

gin rummy, then contract bridge,

followed by a nap.

Looking for pink buds

to prune back, the *mohel* tends

his flower garden.

Look, Muffy! I've found

the most splendid tchotchke for

our Hanukkah bush.

Scrabble® anarchy

after *putzhead* is placed on

a triple-word score.

The curved greenish twig

is a snake! Time to go back

to our hotel room.

BLT on toast—

the rabbi takes his first bite,

then the lightning bolt.

Jewish and slightly

dyslexic—I thought I was

buying a *Chai* Pet.

Jewish voodoo tip—

mention an acting career,

then watch for chest pain.

The frost-withered fields

flecked with white chrysanthemums—

Bubbeleh, your scarf.

*S*hatner and Nimoy

observing Shabbos—"Scotty,

beam up a minyan."

Our youngest daughter,

our most precious jewel. Hence,

the name Tiffany.

Lightbulb out again—

how many of us must meet

to change it this time?

Seven-foot Jews in

the NBA slam-dunking—

my alarm clock rings.

"Love the stranger, for

you were strangers in Egypt."

Can't we be just friends?

The sparkling blue sea

beckons me to wait one hour

after my sandwich.

Visitors sweat on

plastic-covered sofas saved

for whom? Kissinger?

The wily red fox—

at temple, I spy its paws

lurking in a stole.

Shedding its wet skin,

the spritzing seltzer bubble

becomes a Buddha.

Proof Columbus was

Jewish—kept telling the crew

no running on deck.

Premature pleasure—

savoring the chopped liver

ahead of the guests.

Middle East peace talks—

the parties reach agreement.

Falafel for lunch.

*S*haking a raised fist—

"May a plague enter his gums!"

says the nice old man.

Hava nagila,

hava nagila, hava—

enough already.

$\mathcal{T}$esting the warm milk

on her wrist, she beams—nice, but

her son is forty.

A lovely nose ring—

excuse me while I put my

head in the oven.

Monarch butterfly,

I know your name used to be

Caterpillarstein.

Hidden connection—

starvation in Africa,

food left on my plate.

My nature journal—

today, saw some trees and birds.

I should know the names?

*S*JF seeking

eternal soul mate—must be

a professional.

Like a bonsai tree,

your terrible posture at

my dinner table.

*C*ongratulations

on being first in your class

at Stanley Kaplan.

$\mathcal{T}$ea ceremony—

steam, incense, lacquered bamboo.

Try the cheese danish.

Odd new disorder—

the Jew who mistook his wife

for a yarmulke.

Monet? Van Gogh? *Feh.*

Pissarro—a mensch! Did you

know he was Jewish?

After the warm rain,

the sweet scent of camellias.

Did you wipe your feet?

The spitting image

of her father. Down the road

rhinoplasty, yes?

After the youngest

recites the Four Questions, the

fifth—when do we eat?

Such *nakhes*! Our son,

the hitchhiker, has been named

head of a new cult.

Jews on safari—

map, compass, elephant gun,

hard sucking candies.

Would-be convert lost—

thawed Lender's Bagels made a

bad first impression.

Wet moss on the old

stone path—flat on my back, I

ponder whom to sue.

Filled with guilt about

fly-fishing—offspring of an

interfaith marriage.

The long pilgrimage

to the venerable shrine—

Leonard's of Great Neck.

Too much Seder wine—

I dream of pyramids built

with cubes of sugar.

*Q*uietly murmured

at Saturday services,

Yanks 5, Red Sox 3.

No egg and no cream,

just syrup, seltzer, and milk—

Zen of the egg cream.

*C*oroner's report—

"The deceased, wearing no hat,

caught his death of cold."

$\mathcal{T}$oday I am a

man. Tomorrow I return

to the seventh grade.

The sparrow brings home

too many worms for her young.

"Force yourself," she chirps.

Harry Houdini—

amazing escape from his

real name, Erich Weiss.

Today, mild *shvitzing*.

Tomorrow, so hot you'll *plotz*.

Five-day forecast—*feh*.

Jewish nudist camp,

surgical scars compared—who

did your gall bladder?

The pure white lotus—

how rare to glimpse it parked in

my neighbor's driveway.

"*C*an't you just leave it?"

the new Jewish mother asks—

umbilical cord.

Cherry blossoms bloom.

Sure, it's beautiful, but is

it good for the Jews?

Left the door open

for the Prophet Elijah.

Now our cat is gone.

"Is this bug kosher?"

Davening praying mantis

asks before dining.

The shivah visit—

so sorry for your loss. Now

back to my problems.

Constipation gas

fiber enema—chatting

with the *mishpocheh*.

Now that Koreans

are "the New Jews," the old Jews

can leave for Boca.

Swollen by spring rain,

flowing into inky pools,

the varicose vein.

$\mathcal{Y}$om Kippur—forgive

me, God, for the Mercedes

and all the lobsters.

Jewish Buddhist gripe—

"Threw out my back davening

in the full lotus."

Mom, please! There is no

need to put that dinner roll

in your pocketbook.

Hard to tell under

the lights—white yarmulke or

male-pattern baldness?

Lonely mantra of

the Buddhist monk—"They never

call, they never write."

One of us must be

the designated drinker—

Jewish carousing.

Bare autumn branches,

the old crow sits. Mother, come

down from there at once.

How can I atone

for scalping my tickets to

the High Holidays?

Jewish summer camp—

the tall pines cleared of wildlife

by a sing-along.

Buying sliced nova,

I feel a whole smoked whitefish

giving me a look.

$\mathcal{T}$he Jewish New Year—

in Times Square, no ball is dropped.

Where is everyone?

98
≤
99

Heimlich. Is that a

Jewish name? I wonder, as

a diner turns blue.

*C*oncert of car horns

as we debate the question

of when to change lanes.

Parents in mourning—

how can our own daughter be

dating a drummer?

A haiku poet?

Go ahead. You can always

fall back on teaching.

Denmark's Jewish prince—

"To be or not to be—Oy!

Have I got tsuris."

"Through the Red Sea costs

extra." Israeli movers

overcharge Moses.

"Baby needs a new

mink coat!" Compulsive gambler,

all-night dreidel game.

Manhattan sidewalk—

a Hindu street vendor sells

potato knishes.

$\mathcal{J}$s one Nobel Prize

so much to ask from a child

after all I've done?

Sorry I'm not home

to take your call. At the tone

please state your bad news.

About the Author

DAVID M. BADER is a writer living in New York City, a pursuit that raises the eternal question, "From this he makes a living?" He is not even distantly related to Supreme Court Justice Ruth Bader Ginsburg, though he insists on referring to her as "Aunt Ruth."